MW01267888

SUB-3 HOUR MARATHON PLAYBOOK

PAUL BRADFORD

Copyright © 2022 Paul Bradford
All rights reserved.
ISBN: 979-8-3640-6523-0

DEDICATION

To my girl, Melanie. I love you, always x

To my boys, Euan & Ross. For inspiring me to lead and always be strong x

To my Mum, thanks for everything x

To the man who ignited my passion for personal health & strength,
my late father John Bradford.
The best father, husband, and grandad we could have hoped for.
Dad, you are still here with me every day: "Go for it!"

Disclaimer

This book represents the methods that the author has developed and implemented to achieve his goals. The methods are a combination of the work of others, where the author has selected the parts that worked for him. The ideas represented in this book are not a personal exercise prescription for you and are not intended to be a substitute for the services of a trained healthcare practitioner and may be hazardous. Consult with your health care practitioner before engaging in any diet, nutritional supplement, or exercise regimen. The author disclaims responsibility for any adverse effects resulting directly or indirectly from information contained in this book.

CONTENTS

ACKNOWLEDGMENTS

I am not an expert.
I am someone who reads, asks questions and takes inspiration from others who blaze the trail ahead of me.
I apply the methods that may work for me, and if they do, I share what I have learned from others.
I would like to call out those that I have learned from and been inspired by:

John Bradford:
My late father, and the inspiration behind everything I am proud of in my life.
As a businessman, he taught me the lesson on hard work and its benefits.
As a bodybuilder, he inspired me and my friends in our formative teenage years.
The main lesson I've learned:
"Be Strong, you never know who you might be inspiring"

Bill Pierce, Scott Murr, Ray Moss
Authors of
'Runner's World Run Less, Run Faster: Become a Faster, Stronger Runner with the Revolutionary 3-Runs-A-Week Training Program'.
This is the book that not only inspired me to believe I could run Sub-3, but also provided a proven research-backed process for actually doing it. Much of my method for marathon training is based on their outstanding framework.

Tim Ferriss
Reading the 'Four Hour Work Week' started a revolution in my mind which continues to this day. Tim has a rare ability to deconstruct world-class performance in many fields and explain the essential components of success to the guy in the street.

"Perfection is Achieved Not When There Is Nothing More to Add, But When There Is Nothing Left to Take Away" - Antoine de Saint-Exupery

Lewis Howes
Lewis is headteacher at 'The School of Greatness' podcast and now an author of a book of the same title. His personal story inspires me to think big, follow a process and take action.

Harry Singha

A great man who believes in always 'adding value' first.

His guidance on 'taking imperfect action' has led to breaking through many of the artificial barriers I had placed in the way of my progress.

Bill Hemsworth

Professional Bodybuilder and winner of Mr Britain, Bill owned the Furness Health Studio gym in my hometown, and created a culture that was both welcoming and inspirational.

Every person who works out in Barrow-In-Furness has been influenced by his legacy, whether they realize it or not.

PREFACE

<u>My journey to Sub-3</u>

On a cold bleak afternoon, I waited in line with all the other kids, shivering. The wind whips in from the Irish sea and chills me to the bone. The gun goes off and we set off sprinting across the fields heading towards the beach. Within 400 m my legs feel like lead and my chest is tightening. 200 m later and I have resorted to a run / walk / shuffle technique. This is a miserable place to be. Welcome to the school annual cross-country race. I am 14 and **I am NOT a runner**.

From a young age I was fascinated by bodybuilding, powerlifting and sprinting. All my thoughts and training revolved around these short distance, high-intensity hobbies. My own personal claim to fame was that I won the school 200-meter track race aged 14, which qualified me for the North-West regional championships where I finished dead last. The thought of running any more than 400 m was something that I had no desire to do.

Fast forward 10 years and I have now gone all-in on bodybuilding and weightlifting. I weigh 105 kg and when I first met my new girlfriend (now wife!), in an effort to join-in with her exercise routine, we go out for a run together in Sefton Park, Liverpool. I make it only 200 m and then must stop to catch my breath. This reinforced what I already know - **I am NOT a runner.**

Fast forward 15 years. It 's April 2015 and on a very bleak rainy day in Boston (weather reminiscent of my aforementioned high school cross country experience), at age 39 I cover the 26.2 mile course in two hours 57 minutes 33 seconds. This was also my 5th attempt at going Sub-3, after 5 previously failed attempts.

What followed was the busiest 18 months of my entire professional career. My travel commitments meant I was out of the country 50% of the time. At the organization where I work there are no 'set work hours and the culture is simply to get the job done. There is no clocking-on and clocking-off and I absolutely thrive with this autonomous approach. However, with such a busy schedule, and with a wife and two young boys at home, I faced the very real possibility of putting my amateur athletic pursuits on the back burner.

But the challenges of time management and work-life balance only crystallized my focus to continue to pursue my athletic goals. I still had a fire in my belly to work hard and make progress. With zero spare time in my agenda, every single workout needs to count. Living out of a suitcase, it is critical for me to ruthlessly plan my workouts based on the environment and equipment that I will have access to at my destination.

On 6 November 2016 I travelled out to New York City to run in the world's biggest marathon and once again was able to cover the distance in under three hours, finishing this time in two hours 58 minutes 32 seconds.
For a self -confessed non-runner, this was a victory forged through unwavering belief, commitment to the process and a 100% all-in attitude on race day.

In 2019, I broke 3 hours again with a Personal Best time of 2 hour 56 minutes at the Chicago Marathon, again on a day where the weather posed a real challenge to fast times.

I am proud to say that **now, I am runner**. Not a natural runner, but someone who loves the spiritual feeling of running through a forest trail as the sun comes up. I've tasted the 'Runner's High'...and I'm addicted.

Your journey to Sub-3
If you've told yourself that you are 'NOT a runner', then tell yourself a different story.
If you have ever thought about running a marathon in three hours but felt that it was only for the 'natural runners', I urge you to think again.
If you are somebody that has repeatedly tried to break the three-hour barrier but came up short, I encourage you to refocus and follow a proven strategy and then truly prepare to execute on game day.

Sub-3 is absolutely possible for you.

How? By following the '**Sub-3PB system'**

Why? Because it works

What is it? A 16-week routine of:

3 x Runs
2 x Cross-training sessions
1 x Strength & Conditioning session

Result = Sub-3 marathon

I know that through these pages you will pick up tactics that will help you on your journey and also, I hope that you can avoid some of the potholes that I hit along the way.

For now, it's over to you.
Your time goal is to 2 hours XXmins XXseconds.
You fill in the blanks.
Let's get to work.

Paul

CHAPTER 1
BELIEVE: THE POWER OF MINDSET

"Reality is negotiable"

It is the night before the 2015 Boston Marathon.

I am in the bathroom washing up, and Mel shouts through from the bedroom:

"How are you feeling about Sub-3 tomorrow? Are you nervous?"

Some context on this question:
I have been chasing Sub-3 for years, failing on the previous 4 attempts
We have flown across the Atlantic to be here.
The weather in Boston in terrible, with more heavy rain and strong wins forecast for Raceday.

My response:

"I'm not nervous, I'm excited. Sub-3 is already done"

Whilst my response may appear arrogant, it is not intended that way. It truly reflects how I feel. I am utterly convinced I will run sub-3 tomorrow.
Why?
Because I have already rehearsed it over 100 times on my mind. I know how it feels, I can hear the crowd, I can see the home straight.
Our brains are powerful, and with the right evidence can truly believe in any future outcome. The evidence I am building my belief on:

I have fully committed to a proven training program
My training and warm-up race paces have been consistent with a Sub-3 achievement
I have rehearsed this successful outcome in my mind EVERY DAY for the preceding 3 months.

Imagine yourself at the start line, excited to deliver on your potential, with the absolute certainty that you can do it. That is a rare, and critically important mindset to have.

Ready to train this mindset yourself? Then get crystal clear on what you want to achieve.

Goal Setting

Being laser-focused on your goal is THE essential starting point for acquiring discipline. Without a direction in mind, it is unlikely that we will accomplish anything of significance. That is exactly why I made the first letter of my GREATER results model to be 'G', representing Goal setting. I spend a huge amount of time with my clients focused on this area because it is so critical.

For a tough goal to be achieved it is also vital that you understand your purpose. What is your 'why' for wanting to get to that end point? What will achieving this goal give you? Will your 'why' keep you on-track when times get tough?

For every goal, there are specific strategies that can be adopted to achieve success. In other words, you need to follow a plan. A structured game plan increases your chances of staying on track when temptation arises.

As an example, let's say you want to achieve a qualifying time for the Boston Marathon. There are proven ways of achieving this and it requires putting yourself through some 'character-building' tough workouts.

So, what do you do when you are facing the toughest workout of the week and you are not feeling great? Maybe you didn't sleep so well last night, or it's cold and raining outside. If you genuinely believe in the process you are following, you know that missing that tough workout will reduce your chances of performing on the big day. Keeping your eyes on the prize will keep you moving forward when challenges arise. This is COMMITMENT. There are only two types of commitment: IN or OUT. IN means 100% IN. Anything else (e.g., "I'll see how it goes!") defaults to OUT.

Call to Action Time

Throughout this playbook there are times when it's over the
you to take affirmative action. This is the first 'Call to Action':

Call to Action: Goal Setting (Time allocation: 5 minutes)

Take time to get crystal clear on your goal and understand WHY
this goal is important to you. Write this down.

The proven path to Phenomenal Achievement:

I have developed and successfully applied the **ABBA** framework:

Setting a goal requires **ASPIRATION**
Feeling it requires **BELIEF**
Sharing it requires **BRAVERY**
Achieving it requires **ACTION**

Setting a goal requires ASPIRATION

Aspiration (noun)
a strong desire to achieve something high or great
(Ref: Merriam-Webster dictionary on-line)

The origin of any goal is the aspiration to change from your current status to
a more desirable future state. The dissatisfaction with your current ability,
and aiming for an improvement, is what provides the motivation needed to
achieve Sub-3.
Achieving Sub-3 requires running 6.51 min / mile (4:16 min / mile) or faster
average pace over 26.2miles. If that seems like too tough an ask, then let 's
break it down into smaller parts.
Firstly, be prepared to feel that 6.51 is crazy fast at the beginning of the
training programme. As your body strengthens in response to the tough

9

workouts, your confidence in your abilities will also rise to meet your aspiration. Remember what I told you here! If at any point during the programme you are starting to feel despondent about achieving the required pace on race day, come back to this section again and re-read it! Commit to the programme and you will come into outstanding form.

Secondly, your CURRENT race personal bests will give you an indication of your CURRENT potential marathon time. It is critical that your training is based off your current fitness level to safely make progress over time. Starting your training programme with paces that are too fast for your current ability, will lead to overtraining (at best) or significant injury (at worst)

There are several race predictions tables online. They take your recent race performances over various distances and predict your marathon racing time. It is possible to do a 5km race and predict a marathon finish time. However, it would be more accurate to do a 10km time trial and more accurate still to use a recent half marathon time. To give you an idea of my race times on the run up to my sub-3 races:

5km: 17mins 50seconds
10km: 38mins 30 seconds
Half marathon: 1hr 24mins 30seconds

Call to Action: Marathon Race Prediction Time based on current fitness levels (Time allocation: 5 minutes)

Runner's World have a great on-line Marathon Performance Predictor. Take the time to enter your current race results to estimate your marathon time.

Don't have recent race results? Run a 5 or 10km time trail and upload the time into the predictor.

Ref: www.runnersworld.com

Feeling it requires BELIEF

Belief (noun)
conviction of the truth of some … phenomenon especially when based on examination of evidence

(Ref: Merriam-Webster dictionary on-line)

The pre-Boston discussion outlined above, demonstrates the BELIEF that I had going into the race.

My belief was not unfounded: it was based on objective evidence from my workouts and warm-up race paces, and a daily commitment to mentally rehearsing success at the upcoming event.

This is about commitment to the *process*, which will ultimately lead to success.

Mental conditioning to enhance Belief:

Win the Morning, Win the Day #WTM

I am a huge believer in morning routines. Starting off each day with a predictable regular process sets you up for success on that specific day and keep you on the path to achieve your long-term goals.

Every morning I go through a process of visualizing and verbalizing out-loud the goals that I want to achieve. Example:

"Every day I will make an investment in optimizing my physical, mental, emotional and spiritual wellbeing.
On the 7th of November I will run under 3 hours at the New York City Marathon".

I combine this mantra with physical movement, literally walking around the kitchen saying this with real emotion. I can visualize the achievement happening. I follow off this saying by physically thrusting my fist in the air and shouting "YES!" (Think Rocky Balboa running up the museum steps and thrusting his fist skyward).

Sounds crazy? This is mental conditioning; Belief must start within you. If you can't say what you want to achieve out loud when you are on your own, then believe me, you won't have the belief in yourself when you get to the start line.

Commit to the process.
Condition yourself for success.

There is an important distinction between hoping for success and truly believing it. Let's review this in the next section.

3. Sharing it requires BRAVERY
When you have chosen your race, share it with those who will hold you accountable.
Trust me, there are critical mental changes that take place when you use language that demonstrates intention and belief, rather than vague hope.

"The world makes way for the man who knows where he is going"
Ralph Waldo Emerson

Imagine over hearing 2 people talking about their aspiration for an upcoming marathon:

Person One:
"I hope I can get under 3-hours, if I can. And if I have a good day "
Versus
Person Two:
"I am going Sub-3, no matter what. "

Which statement makes you BELIEVE more: 1 or 2?
I'm sure you agree that statement 2 wins hands-down.
It feels a little uncomfortable saying it with such certainty, doesn't it? Maybe feels like you are bragging...what if you tell everyone you are going to do it, and then you fail? Failure is nothing to be afraid of. Fully commit to the programme and stick to the game plan on race day. Your team will support you no matter what the outcome.
The more you say it, the more you say it with conviction.
The more conviction you have, the more people you share your ambition with.
The more you share it, the more you BELIEVE.
The more success becomes a certainty.

4. Achieving it requires action.
There are a lot of opinions on how to run sub-3. My advice is to follow the guidance of those who have been on a similar journey to yourself and have achieved it.
Following the training advice of a Kenyan runner is simply not applicable for the average club runner. Kenyan 's arguably have a genetic advantage and they most definitely have a cultural advantage when it comes to distance running. If you wanted to become a better swimmer, training exactly like Michael Phelps at his peak is unlikely going to give you the results that you desire.

Ultimately it doesn't matter which programme that you follow so long as it is something that you can fit around your work and family responsibilities, and you commit 100% to it.

The programme that I follow works for me because:

1) It requires only 3 runs per week which fits in around my extensive commitments and reduces my injury risk.
2) It is structured and specific, so the guesswork is taken out.
3) As a very average runner it has helped my progress rapidly.

A note on being anti-social:

Achieving your marathon goal requires you to be **selfish**.

Let me say it again with emphasis:

Achieving **YOUR** marathon goal requires **YOU** to be **SELFISH**.

The workouts are very specific. You won't be able to meet up with friends to go for a 'jog' in-lieu of your specific-pace long run. 4-hour weekend social café-bike rides are put on hold until after the marathon. If you have a training partner also going for Sub-3 (and ideally is a little faster than you) then that is perfect! You will inspire each other to stay disciplined and hunt down that big goal.

Mindset Summary

One quote encapsulates every aspect of the successful mindset approach:

"Make mistakes of ambition and not mistakes of sloth. Develop the strength to do bold things, not to suffer."

Niccolò Machiavelli

Call to Action: Mindset (Time allocation: 10 minutes)

"You are doing the marathon! What time are you aiming for?"

A common question amongst runners.

On a piece of paper, write down your response and commitments:

- How will you answer the above question about your goal time for your upcoming race? Consider the words and HOW you emphasize them
- What are your daily commitments to training your mind to BELIEVE you can achieve Sub-3?
- Who will you share your Sub-3 ambition with? Start small, choose 3 people.

- Note: this should feel a little scary. That's how you know you are doing it right.

CHAPTER 2
SUB3 PB SYSTEM OVERVIEW

The workouts that provided the right combination for all my successful Sub-3 attempts are captured in the Sub-3 PB system, comprising a weekly routine of:

3 x Run workouts
2 x Cross-training sessions
1 x Strength & Conditioning session

3 Run workouts per week is lighter than many other marathon training schedules. Having tried others that required 5-6 days of run training per week, I simply went backwards in my performance, arriving jaded at the start line of my race. I was undoubtedly fit; however, I was not fresh or fast.

That is when I discover the FIRST training system, and with some personal modifications, applied it with great success. Sub-3 PB was born!

How workouts are sequenced matters, and the optimal weekly routine I have found is:

Monday	Tuesday	Wednesday	Thursday	Friday	Saturday	Sunday
Strength & Conditioning Session	Run : Intervals	Cross-Training Session #1	Run : Tempo	Cross-Training Session #2	Run : Long Run	Rest / Active Recovery

This weekly routine reflects the key elements of the programme:
The Key (Priority) workouts are the runs
Arrive at each Key Run workout fresh so can nail the intended session, and allow 48 hours recovery between each run
The Cross-training and Strength & Conditioning sessions are supplementary to the Key Run workouts, and therefore should not compromise your ability to deliver each run session. By having the Key Run and Supplementary workouts on different days, you achieve this objective.

We will walk through each type of workout over the next chapters.

CHAPTER 3
3 X RUNS PER WEEK

My method is based on 3 specific runs per week:
1. Interval run
2. Tempo run
3. Long run

In simple terms:
1. Interval run = short distances FASTER than race-pace
2. Tempo run = medium distances CLOSE to race-pace
3. Long run = longer distances slightly SLOWER than race-pace

INTERVAL RUNS

Interval runs are high intensity repeats of distances between 400m and 1600m, carried out faster than race pace. These will improve your VO2 max, which is a measurement of your aerobic physical fitness and is an important determinant of endurance capacity during prolonged exercise.
VO2max = Volume Oxygen Maximum = the maximum amount of oxygen that can be taken up, transported and utilized by the body per minute. It is measured in milliliters per kilogram of body weight per minute (ml/kg/min) and generally tested by running on a treadmill whilst wearing a facemask that is connected to a ventilation machine. All other factors being equal, an athlete with a higher V02 max will be able to outperform an athlete with a lesser measurement in an endurance event owing to their higher effectiveness of oxygen utilization.
It is not necessary to have your VO2 max tested as part of marathon preparation, and it is sufficient to know that high intensity interval runs will assist in increasing your VO2 max.

Structure of interval sessions:
Warm-up: 15-minute building-pace jog before commencing intervals
3 x 30 seconds faster paces intervals (spirited but sub-maximal efforts) with 30 seconds recovery between each one.

Recovery between Intervals: 2 min recovery walk / jog between intervals (keep moving!)
Cool-Down: 5-10 minute easy jog and stretches

Interval run summary:
Interval distances: numerous repeats of 400m-1600m (1 mile)
Pacing: Significantly faster than race pace
Total distance per session:
5000m / 3miles at intensity plus approx. 3 miles of warm up / recovery / cool own
Frequency: ONCE per week

TEMPO RUNS

Tempo runs are carried out around marathon race pace, or quicker, and focus on increasing your lactate threshold. During intense activity, working muscles will produce waste products (such as lactic acid, which is believed to cause the burning sensation in the muscles) that will ultimately limit your ability to continue. Tempo workouts specifically train your body to efficiently manage these chemicals so that you can train for longer at higher intensities (referred to as increasing your 'Lactate Threshold').

Think of lactate production as water pouring into a bucket that has a hole in the bottom. At low exercise intensities the flow of the lactate (the water) flowing into your muscles (the bucket) is so slow that the water leaks out the hole in the bottom (this is your ability to remove lactate from the working muscle) and the bucket does not fill up. When training above threshold, the lactate (water) is produced so quickly that even allowing for the hole in the bucket, the bucket fills and overflows. This imbalance means that the body will have to stop exercising in order to stop the lactic acid production flooding the working muscle.

The goal is to have a bigger hole in your bucket, so that at high intensities when the lactate production ramps up, it is efficiently cleared from the muscle. To create this improved filtration system, it is critical that an athlete trains at threshold intensity, which will be at race pace or faster. Tempo runs range from 3 miles up to 10 miles (5km to 16km).

Structure of Tempo sessions:
Warm-up: 15 minute building-pace jog before commencing intervals
3 x 30 seconds faster paces intervals (spirited but sub-maximal efforts) with 30 seconds recovery between each one.
Main set: complete as prescribed in the 16-week plan
Cool-Down: 5-10 minute easy jog and stretches

Tempo run summary:
Distances: Range between 3 miles and 10 miles (5km-16km)

Pacing: At, or faster than, race pace
Frequency: ONCE per week

LONG RUN

The once weekly long run is carried out at a pace slower than race pace and is aimed at building running resilience, efficiency & economy. Think about this when you are on the freeway, and you only have a small amount of gas left in the tank. Your display tells you there is only 10miles left in the tank, and the nearest gas station is 15 miles away. What do you do to make sure you can make it? You slow down to get better gas efficiency. You may even notice that the 'distance to empty' has gone up. 10 miles, 11 miles, 15 mikes, 17miles. This is the same principle that we apply to the long run: cover the same distance by using less fuel. Long runs range from 13 miles up to 20 miles. (21km to 32km).

How long does the long run need to be?

My best race performances have been with maxing out the long runs at 20 miles (32km).

But that's 6 miles shorter than the race! Is that enough?

Remember your goal: To run Sub-3 on Raceday.
Your goal is NOT to run 26 miles in training and exponentially increase your risk of fatigue (best-case scenario) or injury (worst-case scenario).
It's true that this is shorter than the race distance. However, your weekly cumulative distance from your 3 weekly runs, plus other cross-training, will get you to the start line fresh, confident and ready.
I've ran up to 24 miles (38.5km) on long runs in the past, and I've paid the price. Learn from my mistakes:
Run less, run faster.

Long runs are the closest simulation to actual race day, so therefore are a great opportunity to simulate race-day routines.

Example:

Let's say your race starts at 09:00am.
On your Long Run training day, you can practice:
Setting up at the same time as you plan on Raceday
Wearing the same clothes and running shoes as you plan on Raceday
Eating your pre-race breakfast as you plan on Raceday
Practice in-race fueling as you plan on Raceday
Record how you feel, and your pacing
In short, when you get to the actual Raceday, everything that you need to do is familiar.

Structure of Long Run session

Warm-up: 5 minutes mobilizations and 5 min jog to loosen muscles

Main Set: Execute prescribed distance and pace. For the faster sessions, the prescribed speed may feel too fast initially. Your goal is to hit the average pace over the entire session, so expect that your first few miles are below the prescribed average. I suggest aiming to hit the required average pace by the halfway point, and then maintain the average on the way back to the start.

Cool-Down: 5-10 minute easy jog and stretches. I aim to reach my target distance 5 minutes away from home, and stop my watch, allowing a gentle cool down to reach my front door.

Recovery: Complete rest or active recovery is required the following day for the body to absorb the long run stress. **VIP:** Active recovery is NEVER a run. Choose another way to mobilize the body such as bike, swim or walking.

Long Run summary:
Long run distances: 13 to 20miles
Pacing: All slower that marathon race pace (+15 seconds to +60 seconds per mile)
Total distance per session:
Frequency: ONCE per week

The 16-week programme

None of the runs could be classed as easy and there are certainly no recovery runs. Therefore, a diligent approach to PREPARE and RECOVER from each session is CRITICAL.

NEVER run consecutive days, thereby allowing a minimum of 48 hours rest between run sessions, and my preferred order of runs is as follows:
Tuesday - Interval Run
Thursday - Tempo Run
Saturday - Long Run

On the next pages you will find the **Sub-3 PB** 16-week plan in both statute and metric distances.

Sub-3 16-week plan STATUTE DISTANCES

	Run 1 INTERVALS	Run 2 TEMPO	Run 3 LONG
Week 16	3 x 1600m	6 mile total (2 miles @ 5km pace in middle)	13 miles @ MP + 30s/mile
Week 15	4 x 1200m	7 miles total (4 miles @ MP in middle)	15 miles @ MP + 45s/mile
Week 14	5 x 1km	8 miles total (6 miles @ MP in middle)	18 miles @ MP+60s/mile
Week 13	8 x 800	9 miles total (6 miles @ HMP in middle)	20 miles @ MP+60s/mile
Week 12	12 x 400m	10 miles total (5 miles @ MP in middle)	16 miles @MP + 45s/mile
Week 11	3 x 1600m	8 miles total (6 miles @ HMP in middle)	20 miles @ MP+45s/mile
Week 10	4 x 1200m	10 miles total (5 miles @ 10km pace in middle)	13 miles @ MP+15s/mile
Week 9	5 x 1km	8 miles total (5 miles @ MP in middle)	18 miles @ MP+30s/mile
Week 8	8 x 800m	8 miles total (5 miles @ 10km pace in middle)	20 miles @ MP+30s/mile
Week 7	12 x 400m	10 miles @ MP	18 miles @ MP+30s/mile
Week 6	3 x 1600m	8 mile total (3 miles @ 5km pace in middle)	20 miles @ MP+30s/mile
Week 5	4 x 1200m	10 miles @ MP	18 miles @ MP+30s/mile
Week 4	5 x 1km	8 miles @ MP	20 miles at MP+15sec/ mile
Week 3	8 x 800m	5 miles @ HMP Pace	13 miles @ MP
Week 2	12 x 400m	6 mile total (2 miles @ 5km pace in middle)	10 miles @ MP
RACE WEEK!	6 x 400 (max!)	2 Miles @ MP	RACE DAY!
Comments	This workout can be substituted for an athletic club interval session	Stay disciplined to your target paces OR this workout can be substituted for a local 3-6 mile (5-10km) race or cross-country event	Track your AVERAGE pace throughout. First 2 miles can be slower paced to act as a warm-up.

Sub-3 16-week plan METRIC DISTANCES

	Run 1 INTERVALS	Run 2 TEMPO	Run 3 LONG
Week 16	3 x 1600m	10km total (3kms @ 5km pace in middle)	21 km @ MP + 20s/km
Week 15	4 x 1200m	11km total (6km @ MP in middle)	24 km @ MP + 30s/km
Week 14	5 x 1km	13km total (10km @ MP in middle)	29 km @ MP+40s/km
Week 13	8 x 800	14km total (10km @ HMP in middle)	32 km @ MP+40s/km
Week 12	12 x 400m	16km total (8km @ MP in middle)	26 km @MP + 30s/km
Week 11	3 x 1600m	13km total (10km @ HMP in middle)	32 km @ MP+30s/km
Week 10	4 x 1200m	16km total (8km @ 10km pace in middle)	21 km @ MP+10s/km
Week 9	5 x 1km	13km total (8km @ MP in middle)	29 km @ MP+20s/km
Week 8	8 x 800m	12km total (8km @ 10km pace in middle)	32 km @ MP+20s/km
Week 7	12 x 400m	16km @ MP	29 km @ MP+20s/km
Week 6	3 x 1600m	13km total (5km @ 5km pace in middle)	32 km @ MP+20s/km
Week 5	4 x 1200m	16km @ MP	29 km @ MP+20s/km
Week 4	5 x 1km	13km @ MP	32 km at MP+10sec/km
Week 3	8 x 800m	8km @ HMP Pace	21 km @ MP
Week 2	12 x 400m	10km total (3km @ 5km pace in middle)	16km @ MP
RACE WEEK!	6 x 400 (max!)	3km @ MP	RACE DAY !
Comments	This workout can be substituted for an athletic club interval session	Stay disciplined to your target paces OR this workout can be substituted for a local 3-6 mile (5-10km) race or cross-country event	Track your AVERAGE pace throughout. First 3km can be slower paced to act as a warm-up.

KEY

MP	Predicted Marathon Pace
HMP	Predicted (or measured) Half Marathon Pace
5km Pace	Predicted (or measured) 5km Pace
10km Pace	Predicted (or measured) 10km Pace

To determine Predicted Times per distance : *Google search for 'runners world race time predict*

CHAPTER 4
2 X CROSS TRAINING SESSIONS

The second part of my Sub-3 PB system is the incorporation of 2 x high intensity cross training (XT) sessions per week. Many traditional marathon running programs would advocate more running sessions per week, often 5-6 days of training. For mere mortals like myself, I simply don't recover between workouts to fully complete the next workout. Not only that but it is also well documented that increasing the mileage through pounding the pavement has a strong correlation with increased injury risk.

My preferred XT method is bike work, and these sessions are mostly done on an inside turbo trainer.

There is a high cross-over of benefit from Bike to Run Fitness meaning your running performance can improve through supplementary bike training, without the additional excessive strain on the body that can come through additional run sessions / mileage.

Home Cycling Workouts:
When at home I historically used a 'turbo trainer' attached to a road / racing bike. With the arrival of more sophisticated home cycling equipment, turbo trainers can now be picked up very cheap. They are not fancy, but they do the job!

I have now invested in a quality home system, the Wattbike Atom (www.wattbike.com). This gives a reproducible way to measure my output through measuring Power (measured in Watts).

A final alternative is to just grab a bike and head outside, finding a hill where you can repeat some intervals. It's about the training stimulus that you deliver, not the equipment that you do it on. Your body doesn't care!

For guiding you throughout the home XT session, there are many on-line platforms you can use. I use Wattbike Hub and Zwift.

Business Travel Cycling Approach

Because of my international travel schedule, these are often the most difficult sessions to fit in owing to the variable quality of stationary bike equipment in hotels.

Above is the hotel gym where I cross-trained for my Sub-3 attempts (respect to the team at my home-from-home Holiday Inn Arena Towers, Amsterdam). A basic range of equipment, however all you need to supplement your Key Run sessions. In fact, the only equipment I use is the bike, with run workouts completed outside unless the weather is so bad that it is unsafe. As a flat country, the Netherlands has no hills to disrupt the wind and it's common to be too windy to safely run outside. That's when the treadmill calls!

To keep the focus, I follow pre-recorded bike sessions from YouTube. Simply search YouTube for '1 hour Cycling Workout' and follow the on-screen instructions. If you can find them, I have successfully used Sufferfest Angels (~60 minutes) and Sufferfest ISLAGIATT (~2 hours).

Assuming that most hotel-gym cycles do not have a reliable way to show Power output, I recommend using a Rating of Perceived Exertion Scale (RPE).

The RPE scale relies on you to rate your own effort on a 10 point scale:

1 = Very low effort
5 = Moderate Effort
7 = 'Threshold' = Effort you could sustain for an hour, no more!
10 = Maximal effort

Your target RPE over the 1-hour session is in an average of 7, with a range from 6-9 as the YouTube video dictates. The intensity of this session is high, with sustained intervals at threshold level. Whilst the workouts vary in duration, I have found the perfect duration to be 60 minutes in weeks 1-7 of the program, with <u>one</u> Weekly XT session extending to 2 hours in the weeks 8-16.

The XT session should not be so long or intense that you carry fatigue into your next Key Run session, thereby compromising your Key Run performance. If anything, the 'cross-training' effect should help you absorb the previous Key Run session and prepare you for the next key run session of the week.

Alternatives for the XT sessions:

Swimming: a first-class way to train the cardiovascular system without further taxing the legs. Whilst many folks are unconfident in their swimming ability, counterintuitive as this may sound, the worse your technique is, the more you fight with the water, and the greater the cardio-vascular training effect.

Stationary Rower: excellent cardio-vascular training effect without the pounding of running. Time-efficient: you can achieve great training effects in a short space of time.

XT summary:
Duration: 60-120 mins
Frequency: TWICE per week
Intensity: Average of RPE 7 for the session

CHAPTER 5
1 X STRENGTH & CONDITIONING SESSION

I was born in the 1970's but I am really a 1980's kid.
I loved watching Arnold and Stallone in action. I could not even guess how many times I've watched Sly training in Siberia in Rocky IV. "If he dies, he dies...". Love it.
Growing up in a bodybuilding household it is no coincidence that I got into weightlifting back then and still lift today.
I have been on a long journey with weightlifting, from the starting point of just wanting big guns for the beach, to where I am now which is using 'Strength & Conditioning' (S&C) sessions to augment my other athletic hobbies, namely running and triathlon.
My philosophy on weight training has evolved significantly from its start point to where it is today:

Strength is a critical success factor in performance enhancement for the endurance athlete.

S&C is often referred to helping 'reduce injury risk'. Whilst I do agree with this, my experience is that S&C work is primarily a *performance enhancer*, with an added side benefit of providing reduced injury risk.

My background is in bodybuilding, where the 'go hard or go home 'approach is widespread. My historical mindset:
"If your muscles are not sore the next day then you haven't trained hard enough!"
This high intensity training is critical to deliver a large enough stimulus to cause hypertrophy (muscle growth).
However, this methodology is detrimental to the endurance athlete, as the DOMS (Delayed Onset Muscle Soreness) that can accompany hard weight training will negatively impact your Key running workouts.
Over many years I have now optimized the balance between strength and running speed.
After following a new programme, inspired by Tim Ferriss '4 Hour Book, I've been able to add 15% to my 1 Rep Max (1RM) Bench Press and 20% to my 1RM Deadlift, in just 6 weeks. (1RM = the maximum weight that you can lift for 1 repetition)
At the same time, I was able to continue to improve my running speed and endurance as I prepared for the Boston Marathon. In the same 6-week period of strength gains, my 5km run time improved from 19.35 to 18.40.

Test	Initial Testing	Re-test at 6 weeks	Change from initial testing
Bench Press	96kg (211lbs)	110kg (242 lbs.)	+14kg = +15%
Deadlift	108kg (238lbs)	130kg (287lbs)	+22kg = +20%
5km run time	19min 35sec	18min 40 sec	-55sec = -5%

My bodyweight remained steady during this period at 76kg (168lbs, or 12 stone exactly).

Tim Ferriss was introduced to this workout by US Track coach, Barry Ross, whose athletes include 200m Olympic Gold medalist, Allyson Felix.
The basic principle is that you deliver a sub-maximal stimulus (2-3 reps of 85-95% of your 1RM poundage) to the muscles, which results in strength gains but without DOMS. As the eccentric part of the movement contributes most significantly to DOMS, this portion is avoided where possible (see notes on deadlift technique). After this sub maximal lift, a plyometric movement (where the elasticity of the muscles is used to produce a greater power output) with the same muscle groups is carried out.

Sounds complicated? It 's not. Here is the routine:

	Exercise	Set 1	Rest	Set 2
	10 minute warm-up			
Superset #1	>Partial Deadlift	85% 1RM x 3reps	5 mins	95% 1RM x 3 reps
	>10m sprints	10m sprints x 3reps		10m sprints x 3
Superset #2	>Bench Press	85% 1RM x 3 reps	5 mins	Repeat Set 1
	>Clapping Press ups	Clapping Press-ups x 6 reps		
	>Bench Twists	Bench Twists : 3 sec hold each side until failure		
Superset #3	>Weighted Pull Ups	85% 1RM x 3 reps	5 mins	Repeat Set 1
	>Face pulls	TheraBand Face Pulls x 12		

Superset #1: Partial Deadlifts > Sprints

Partial Deadlift

Start　　　　　　　　　Top　　　　　　　　　Drop

The bar is raised from the floor as in the traditional deadlift technique, but as the bar reaches knee height the bar is dropped to the floor. This partial movement involves only the concentric part of the movement (the upwards movement) but avoid the DOMS-inducing eccentric movement (the lowering movement under tension).

Sprints : Simply approximate 10m and sprint x3 flat-out after each set of deadlifts.

Superset #2: Bench Press > Clapping Press-ups > Bench Twists

Bench Press

Clapping Press-up

Bench Twist

Superset #3: Weighted Pull Ups > Face pulls

Weighted Pull Ups

Face Pulls

That's it! 45 minutes in total.

You should feel fired up, rather than fatigued. Barry Ross has his athletes perform a track session after this strength session, so as you can imagine it should not take too much out of you!

This minimalist approach to Strength training is ideal for the busy working athlete who wants to find the optimum balance between strength and endurance training.

Further guidance and video demonstrations can be found at www.paulbradfordcoaching.com/resources

S&C summary:
Duration: 45 mins (including Warm-up and Cool-down)
Frequency: ONCE per week
Intensity: 85-95% of 1RM for Bench Press and Deadlift (If you are sore the next day you did too much!)

(All training photographs taken by our Creative Director **Euan Bradford**)

PROUD TO REPRESENT STRYKER (EVENT SPONSOR)
IN BOSTON 2015

THE PATH TO SUCCESS IS NEVER SMOOTH:
5 MARATHONS TO LEARN FROM BEFORE SUB-3 SUCCESS IN
BOSTON 2015

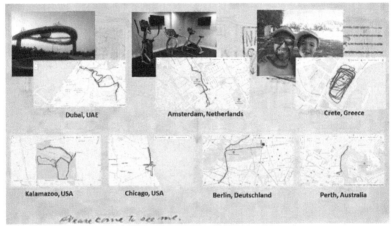

TRAINING ON THE ROAD:
COMMITTED TO THE PROCESS

FATE? RACE NUMBER #3333 @NYC MARATHON 2016…
IN THE HARDEST RACE I HAVE EVER RUN, SUB-3 IS THE **ONLY**
OPTION

CHAPTER 6
MARGINAL GAINS = FREE SPEED

Whilst it may seem that obvious that run training is required to prepare for a marathon, I have determined 4 additional Hidden Key Success Factors that undoubtedly contributed to my Sub-3 success. They are:

- Ruthless Planning
- Recovery
- Nutrition
- Race Weight

Welcome to the world of Marginal Gains, getting 1% better here, and 1% better there. These gains compound together to save minutes on race day and may make the difference to you sneaking in under the 3 hour mark. Welcome to gaining Free Speed.

RUTHLESS PLANNING

"I don't have enough time!"

The common challenge that unites all enthusiastic amateur athletes: *Time.* Or rather, *the perceived lack of time.*

The common amount of time we ALL have, that unites us all: *24 hours a day.*

What is uncommon? Those making progress in key areas of their life prioritize tasks and allocate time accordingly.

Success at Sub-3 requires a time commitment.

Through years away from home on business travel, I have had to adapt my training to make it work around flights, time zones and meetings.

Scheduling your plan is critical to staying on track.

This program requires a maximum of 8 hours training hours per week, with an average of 5.5 hours.
It's that simple. Depending on work and travel commitments, my Monday to Friday workouts were all completed early in the morning so as not to disrupt the family or work. The only impact on the family was the weekend

long run, which tops out at 2 hours 30 mins (20 miles) and again is best done early in the morning.

My single biggest planning learning:

Win the Morning #WTM

Training when the world is sleeping works because it's the time when the world has no expectations of me. No meetings, phone calls, instant messages to reply to…
Each Sunday, I plan for the week, scheduling all commitments in my diary.
My workouts are scheduled, with adequate buffer time around the workout to wake up, shower, refuel etc. before engaging in non-training commitments.

An important note to those who identify themselves as "not a morning person":
Up to my late 20s I would train after work between 5 and 6pm. Increasing work commitments meant that my ability to get to the gym on a regular basis after work was inconsistent. I shifted to training pre-work and after a week of discomfort caused by the early-alarm, my body-clock adjusted, and the benefit was fantastic!
Firstly, I started the day with an immediate win as I achieved an important investment in my health. Contrast that to ending a full working day, leaving no time or energy to train, and slumping into bed with a nagging feeling of guilt that I did not get physically better today. No matter how busy the day gets, I also have a tick in the box of physical progress from my morning workout.
Additionally, endorphins (the feel-good hormone) are released during physical activity. So, after training, when I arrived at work, I was mentally sharp and ready to attack the day.
As I transitioned to Ironman training, which peaks at around 18 hours per week, there is simply no way to successfully achieve this, and be a great spouse and parent, by training exclusively 'after-work'
All these benefits have shown me the benefit of Ruthless Planning and Morning Training.

#WTM works

RECOVERY

The best athletes know when to rest

All athletes have no problem training hard. However, the **best athletes,** the top 5%, are well-rested coming into a workout, can deliver on the objective of the workout, and recover after the workout in preparation for the next session.

Key components of recovery:

Sleep
Nutrition
Soft-tissue work (massage)
Ice-baths

SLEEP

Sleeping well is perhaps the single biggest performance enhancer for the average person on the street. What works for me:
No caffeine after 5 pm
Regular sleep pattern.
Read before bed

No caffeine after 5 pm, has really help me, both with sleep quality and reducing the need to go to the bathroom in the night. Caffeine tolerance varies between individuals; however, a universal impact is that it's a diuretic and thereby increases the frequency of bathroom visits during the night when consumed late evening.

The required amount of sleep is very individual, and I have found that having a regular bed and wake time to be more productive than my hitting a prescribed number. Lights out by 10pm and get up 05:30 works just fine for me.

NUTRITION

After years of hard lessons, I have now landed on a predictable nutritional approach to enhance my performance.
In a hectic life, the big nutrition win is having a solid, predictable routine.

Day in, day out...Rinse and Repeat.

Pre-workout nutrition:
As workouts are all in the morning, they are done fasted. The one exception is the weekly long run, where I train my stomach by simulating my Raceday nutritional approach.
So, rise, hit a quick expresso and head out the door!

Post-workout nutrition:
On returning from any workout, before hitting the shower, I consume:
500 mls water
25g Whey Protein
1 Banana
(+ 100g Maltodextrin after the weekly long run **only**)

Within an hour of the workout completion, I will eat a solid-food meal to further enhance replenishment of my reserves. An example meal:
3 Scrambled eggs, cooked with Coconut Oil.
40g porridge (80g after the weekly long run)

As the body will still be in deficit for hours after a tough workout, the window for refueling and repair extends long after the session has finished. Therefore, 3 hours after my workout, I will eat again with an additional focus now on reducing the inflammatory process:
40g Porridge
80g Blueberries
150g Skyr Yoghurt
Multi-vitamin / mineral tablets
Omega-3 tablet

SOFT TISSUE WORK

During marathon prep, your muscle and connective tissue work hard. Taking a pro-active approach to getting ahead of soft-tissue niggles can prevent their escalation into season-ending injury.
During the 16 programs, I will visit a massage therapist once per week to aid recovery. Scheduling is important, and I have found the most beneficial day for recovery is to hold this appointment 1-2 days after my weekly long run.
It's also extremely valuable to keep on top of the soft-tissue condition through working at home with a foam roller. Simply work the foam roller

through you muscles until you find a 'tight hot-spot' (you will yelp when you find it!) and carefully work over this area for a few minutes or until the intensity of the discomfort subsides.

Yoga is also a great adjunct to soft-tissue repair and mobility enhancement. There are many videos on YouTube that can meet your current physical condition and available time.

ICE BATHS

I have found particular recovery benefit in taking an ice bath after the weekly long run.

Nothing fancy is needed: I simply take used 3 x 1-litre ice cream plastic containers, fill them will water, and put them in the freezer. After the next long run, they are ready and waiting.

Fill your bath with cold water from the tap, put your homemade iceblocks in, and you are ready to go!

I stay in for 10 minutes, ensuring that my legs are submerged, and then grab a warm shower.

RACE WEIGHT

As a rough rule of thumb, assuming all other variables are kept constant, one minute of time can be saved over the marathon distance, for every pound of bodyweight dropped.

In one of my earlier, failed Sub-3 attempts, I calculated after the race that by dropping 6lbs of bodyweight, I could have gained 6 minutes. This would comfortable have gained me a 'Good for age' slot at the London Marathon and had me within sprinting distance of breaking the sub 3hr mark. And I know for certain that if I'm on the home straight with the race clock showing 2:59, I would have found an extra gear for that sprint!

Less chocolate, more coconut water!

MARGINAL GAINS = FREE SPEED

CHAPTER 7
RACE DAY ESSENTIALS

This is it.
All the months of preparation.
It all comes down to today.

This is where your destiny is made.

After many marathon attempts, I have crystalized my race-day essential lessons to 3:

1) Course knowledge is critical
2) Have a game plan
3) Your sports-watch lies

COURSE KNOWLEDGE IS CRITICAL

Unless you train on your intended marathon course, you must prepare yourself with course knowledge long before the race start.
The understanding specifics of the sections, hills and congested areas lead to a race day strategy that provides conservation of energy in places and 'free-speed' in others.
Most major marathon events provide a course map, with details of the elevation gain on hills. Additionally, at the Expo that day before the event, are course-familiarization sessions. These are free gold so go and pay attention!
Additionally, guidance can be sought from someone who has prior course knowledge. I would advise anyone thinking off doing a course to seek out someone who has done it before. This resulting refinement of your strategy could very well make the difference between Sub-3 or missing out by seconds.
If it is a hilly course, you should seek out hills in your long runs. Simulate race day regularly.

HAVE A GAME PLAN

Using the course knowledge gained in Step 1, you can now build a simple and actionable gameplan. The 2 key components of which are (1) Pacing and (2) Nutrition.

Pacing is the most important metric you should track. Most marathons have a bunched start, so it is possible that it will be slow for the first 2 miles. Don't panic! You still have 24 miles to claw back the time.

The big challenge is to hold back at the start. You will be tapered, full of nervous adrenaline and may want to race off like a rocket! Making it worse, you may be surrounded by people feeling the same! Let them go and run your own race. This discipline will pay off when you hit the 24-mile marker feeling strong.

Here is my pacing for Sub-3 at New York Marathon 2016:

 **Paul Bradford**

Bib: 3333

Finish: 02:58:23 | 12:50 PM

START	**00:00:00** (9:51 AM)
5K (3.1mi)	**00:21:20** (10:13 AM)
10K (6.2mi)	**00:41:32** (10:33 AM)
15K (9.3mi)	**01:01:34** (10:53 AM)
20K (12.4mi)	**01:21:56** (11:13 AM)
HALF (13.1mi)	**01:26:30** (11:18 AM)
25K (15.5mi)	**01:43:15** (11:35 AM)
30K (18.6mi)	**02:03:45** (11:55 AM)
35K (21.7mi)	**02:25:16** (12:17 PM)
40K (24.9mi)	**02:48:31** (12:40 PM)
FINISH	**02:58:23** (12:50 PM)

On nutrition, it is key to consider the location of the aid stations and the fuel they will provide. If the race nutrition provider's products have worked for you in training, then you are all set.

If you haven't proven the efficacy of the 'on-course' nutrition with your own body in training, DO NOT try anything new on race day. Bring your own race nutrition. In times of high stress and variability, I advise 'Packing your own Parachute' by bringing your own race fuel.

3) YOUR SPORTS WATCH LIES

To achieve a Sub-3 result, the slowest pace you could average is 6.51 mins / mile. Just one more second slower per mile and you would have missed Sub-3 goal by 3 seconds.

I learned a hard lesson at the New York marathon, where there was a mismatch between the pace and distance covered that my Sports-watch was displaying and what the course markings were telling me. Why? I started my watch too early when I hear the start gun. The Chip time is the official race time you will receive, not the Gun time.

START YOUR WATCH AS YOU CROSS THE TIMING MAT = CHIP TIME
DO NOT START IT AS THE START GUN FIRES

At the 16-mile marker I had averaged 6:38 min / mile, slightly ahead of my pacing plan, as I knew that the course profile would lead to slower pacing in the last 10 miles. No sweat, this was part of the plan.

However, over the next few miles, my average pace continued to drop and after a dreadful patch between mile 23 and 24 it faded to 6.51min/mile. I'd blown it. My form was ragged and slowing. As I entered Central Park, I knew that all this effort would result in a time just seconds over 3 hours.

Then I clocked the official race clock at the 24-mile mark and a quick calculation of the remaining distance meant that I was still on track. It didn't add up. My Garmin says I've blown it, my fatigued brain is doing calculations to say I can do it.

What do to?

I hammered.

I went all in, knowing I had just 15 minutes of suffering to go.

The result was that my official pace was 6.49 min/mile for the 26.2mile course, yet my Garmin measured short at 25.99 miles and 6.51 mins / mile.

This is a critical lesson! Click 'start' on your watch as your cross the timing matt at the start line, not when the horn sounds. Use your Sports-watch as a guide for pacing but also keep your race-head switched on. The finish line is where the organizers put it, not where your sport-watch tells you.

CHAPTER 8
SUMMARY

The Sub-3 hour marathon is won or lost long before the gun goes off, on the lonely pavements around your house.

Believe Sub-3 is possible for you, and then, **do the work**. Fully commit to the Sub-3PB system outlined here.

Once achieved, you will forever have an identity to be proud of as join the Top 5% of all marathon runners. You are a:

Sub-3 Marathoner

No one can ever take this title away from you. But you must **earn it.**

Now, it's over to you.

Your time goal is to **2 hours XXmins XXseconds**.

You fill in the blanks.

Let's get to work.

APPENDIX

Regardless of the outcome of a race, we have the opportunity to learn and improve.

I have written 3 post-marathon race reports:

The first was written after my first unsuccessful attempt to break 3 hours at the Liverpool Marathon in 2014

The other 2 after my successful races at Boston 2015 and New York 2016. Within these posts I cover the key lessons that I learned whilst solving the Sub-3 puzzle, so you can use these lessons without having to learn them for yourself the hard way.

Liverpool Marathon 2014 (Time 3:05.44s)
WRT Blog #004: Every Raceday is a School Day

Hi Guys
I hope you had a great training and racing weekend!
After the big weekend of your season's A-race, it's natural to be reflective.
Your emotions are probably somewhere on the spectrum between ecstasy and depression.
Regardless of how well you did, there is generally a sense of loss. When we have been so consumed by training for an event, that the aftermath can leave us feeling a little lost.
I would suggest taking this immediate post-race period to reflect on your achievements and consider that:

"Every Race Day is a school day! "

I raced at the Liverpool Rock N Roll Marathon on Sunday and took 7 minutes off my previous PB with a time of 3hrs 05 minutes and 44 seconds.

My goals for the 2014 running season were:
1. Break the 3 hour barrier
2. Qualify for London Marathon 2015 'Good for Age 'spot (run under 3 hours 05 minutes)
3. Qualify for Boston Marathon 2015 (run under 3hrs 10 minutes)
I qualified for Boston, missed London by 44 seconds and was 6 lbs. too heavy for a sub 3 run (Too heavy? Why does this matter? See below section on race

weight).
Overall, I 'm pretty happy!

I learned some lessons on Sunday and have detailed these below.

I 'm a simple guy so I like to group my reflections into things that I need to:
START, STOP or CONTINUE.

START

These are often the aspects that you kick yourself for not doing when you look back. I cannot change what has happened but to make things better for next time I would make the following changes:

1. Drop body weight
At 12 stone 2 lbs. (170 lbs. / 77kg) on race morning, I was 6 lbs. (2.7 kg) over my best ever performance-related weight of 11st 10lbs (Ironman 2013). This in because of 2 main reasons: firstly, I was doing nowhere near the training volume of an Ironman but, mostly, because I have been enjoying life too much!
As a rough rule of thumb, approximately 1 minute of time can be saved over the marathon distance, for every pound of bodyweight dropped.
This assumes all other variables are kept constant.
It's a sobering calculation when my 'optimum race weigh would have shaved off 5minutes and 33 seconds, qualified me for a London Marathon 'Good for Age' for 2015 and had me within sprinting distance of breaking the sub 3hr mark.
Less chocolate, more coconut water!

2. Cross-train more
I would usually be in the middle of triathlon training by now, but this season's focus has been exclusively on running. In the past 6 months I can count my bike and swim workouts on one hand. While focus is essential, I get the feeling that the additional fitness derived from cross-training would have benefited my race performance.

STOP

1. Leaving myself with too much to do in the last half of the race.
Pacing is all important in any endurance event, and I consciously held back in the first quarter of the race.
3 hour marathon pace breaks down into 4 x 42min30 sec 10km splits, plus the extra 2.2km.

My first 10km was 45min 05sec, so I was already 2.5 pace.

At halfway the deficit persisted, and my time was 1:3 too much to do in the back half of the race.

There is a great free on-line pace calculator that I u help you calculate your goal splits. Google 'Active Rui

CONTINUE (because it worked)

1. Taper more than I think I need to
My pre-marathon week looked like this:

Monday – Upper Body Strength Work, Core, Foam Roller and Stretches – 45 minutes

Tuesday – 6 miles recovery run with 6 x 100m sprints

Wednesday – 7 miles run @ brisk pace (with 2 miles at Marathon pace 6.49 min/mile between miles 4 and 6)

Thursday – Static Stretches

Friday and Saturday – no training

Sunday – Race Day

That is a really light training week, and work and family commitments stopped me training on Thursday and Friday. Clearly that helped and I felt fantastic on race morning.

2. Eat light on race day!
My bodybuilding past leaves a legacy of over-eating pre-race which has hampered my races in the past.

Today I kept it simple: 40g Porridge oats, sprinkling of dried fruit, spoon of honey and a scoop of whey protein. Cup of tea and lemon water for fluids. All consumed 2 and a half hours out from the start time. This gave ample time for digestion.

The race start was 09:00 and so between 08:00 and 08:30 I drank 500mls of home-brew energy drink (40g Maltodextrin powder with water and cordial). Again, it allowed time for digestion and a quick wee prior to starting. I did have a mild sensation of needing to pee through the race, so I will try bringing the drink forward by 15 minutes next time.

3. Arrive at the race early
I took a direct train to the event, and avoided the unnecessary panic caused by parking and traffic.

I arrived at the race start 90 minutes prior to the race, which allowed time for a bag drop, socializing with fellow Triathlon club comrades and a thorough dynamic warm up.

4. Do a dynamic warm up

thorough 15 minute warm up of increasingly dynamic stretches and
vation drills. I was like a coiled spring after this and had to stop myself
sprinting to the start line!

5. Balance the books

In the week following the race, I have been off-work, and this is a great
opportunity to put family first, training second. My workouts this week have
all been recovery-focused and have consisted of: 1) Wearing compression
tights, 2) Bike rides with the kids for fish and chips, and 3) open water
swimming with Mrs. B to prepare her for her first Olympic distance triathlon
in June.

Until next time.

Be well.

PB. May 28, 2014

Race Report Boston Marathon April 2105 (Time 2:57.33s)

'Sub 3 on 3 runs per week'

Running a sub 3 marathon is a key landmark for any club runner.
While you are never going to challenge the Kenyans, it is a stretch goal for most of us mere mortals.
To put sub-3 into perspective, the mean time for all runners at the 2014 London Marathon was 4:30.45. Running 2:59.59 or quicker would put you in the top 4% of the field!
After 5 previous failed attempts at cracking sub 3 hours, I achieved it at the 2015 Boston Marathon with a time of 2:57.33.
I'm not a natural runner at all and so I wanted to share my marathon training philosophy so that it may provide some guidance for all of us 'enthusiastic amateurs'!

The Process
My approach to training is very simple and is based on the principle of administering a Minimal Effective Dose of training stimulus.
In other words, I aim to get the maximum amount of benefit from the least amount of effort. This is a core principle for efficient achievement in all activities, but it is vital if you are a working parent with an aging body!
So 'Run Less, Run Faster'!
Let's keep it simple – there are only 3 major levers that you can pull to optimize performance. In order of influence:
1. Event-specific fitness
2. Race tactics
3. Race nutrition

1. Event specific fitness
To run sub 3 you will need to hold an average pace of 6.51 per/mile for 26.2 miles, or faster.
There are any numbers of ways to build towards this outcome and I personally prefer the one that maximizes the outcome (run faster) but minimizes the downsides (reduced injury risk and reduced training time commitment).
As such I have used the 3 runs per week approach as promoted by the Runner's World book 'Run less, Run Faster' (Bill Pierce, Scott Murr and Ray Moss).

The method is based on 3 specific runs per week:

1. Interval run
2. Tempo run
3. Long run

Interval runs are high intensity repeats of distances between 400m and 1600m, carried out faster than race pace. These will improve your VO2 max, which is a measurement of your aerobic physical fitness and is an important determinant of endurance capacity during prolonged exercise.

Tempo runs are carried out around marathon race pace, or quicker, and focus on increasing your lactate threshold. During intense activity, working muscles will produce chemicals (namely lactic acid / lactate) that will ultimately limit your ability to continue. Tempo workouts specifically train your body to efficiently manage these chemicals so that you can train for longer at higher intensities.

The weekly long run is carried out at a pace slower than race pace and is aimed at building running strength and a solid endurance base.

These runs are built into a guided 16 week programme, with the pace of each run dictated by your CURRENT (not dream pace!) running ability. This is established by performing a time trial over a set distance, such as a recent race performance.

In addition to the 3 runs, it is recommended to add in 2 high-intensity cardio based cross training workouts (bike, swim, cross-trainer etc.).

My weekly routine looked like this:
Monday – Strength and Conditioning training
Tuesday – Interval run
Wednesday – Bike (Turbo trainer)
Thursday – Tempo Run
Friday – Bike (Turbo trainer)
Saturday – Rest and Family Time
Sunday – Long Run

Maximum training hours per week was 8 hours, with an average of 5.5 hours. It 's that simple. Depending on work and travel commitments, my Monday to Friday workouts were all completed early in the morning so as not to disrupt the family or work. The only impact on the family was the weekend long run, which tops out at 2hours 30mins (20 miles) and again is best done early in the morning.

Saturday is 100% family prime time.

Other considerations for running fitness:

Injury
I went into this Marathon training block carrying a 2 year old Achilles injury. I was realistically thinking this problem would be the end of my running hobby, however with great physio advice on self-management from expert Andrew Caldwell (https://active-therapy.com/), the problem improved during the run up to the Marathon. Andrew has over 20 years of experience and is a consultant for the PGA (Professional Golf Association).
My advice is to see a good Physio as soon as you think you have a problem. It's critical that your therapist understands your running goals. Telling you not to run for 6 months is quite simply not an option!

Training intensity
Be prepared, this programme is tough. The specified paces are much faster that other programs that use moderate paces and higher weekly volume. I consistently found the toughest sessions to complete on my own were the Interval runs. As such, when possible, I attended the Tuesday night interval sessions with Wallasey Athletic Club, under the watchful eye of Coach Dave Walton (You always run faster when you know Dave is watching you 😊). The element of competitive encouragement at these sessions helped me deliver a much greater training stimulus.

Race your way into form
For the same reason that interval sessions are more productive when performed in a group, racing also helps you dig deeper than when you are doing solo tempo runs. I ran cross-country over the winter for the first time ever and this, with a couple of 5km Park Runs thrown in, really helped to sharpen by running. It was also really motivating to run with friends at Wallasey Athletic Club.

2. Race tactics
With a recent best time of 3:05.44, I needed to find a big chunk of time to hit my Sub-3 goal. Like any scary goal, it's critical to step back, use perspective and break it down. A 5.45 minute reduction in time only amounts to a 3% improvement.
Keeping the levers of fitness and nutrition constant, is it possible to find a 3% improvement through tactics alone?
I really think it is, as I've messed up tactics several times previously and failed to deliver the true result that I have worked so hard to achieve.
Previously, I've overcooked the first half of the marathon as I got too competitive. Result: blew up in the last 2 miles and walked home (3 hours 12 mins)

reaction, at my next serious sub 3 attempt, I then ran a very
33 for the first 13.1 miles, thinking I could negative split in the
sult: I did negative split but left myself too much to do on
rs 5mins).

My tactics for Boston were to run the first half slightly faster than 3 hour pace, giving some slack for the inevitable slowing in the second half. I crossed halfway at 1:27.38 (6.40 min / mile pace), with the second half completed in 1:29.55. This felt right and was the easiest (and fastest!) marathon I have ever run. My advice is to have a pacing plan and stick to it – DO NOT SABOTAGE YOUR OWN RACE!

As I left the hotel on race morning, Mel's words were ringing in my ears 'Stick to the plan – don't screw it up!"

Run the race that you have trained for, not the one that you feel you can run on race day. If you are having a great day, remember that 26.2miles is a long way – stick with the plan. The race doesn't begin until mile 20, so if you are still feeling great at this point then go for it!

3. Race nutrition
After really struggling with race nutrition in longer triathlon races, I have been searching for a solution that optimizes performance but minimizes the risks to long term health.
As I eat a mostly a low-sugar diet, my body struggles when I consume high sugar race fuel and gels.
Over the past couple of years I have been experimenting with fueling less and less for training. Except for my long run, the other 5 workouts of the week are done fasted (on an empty stomach). This works because I train in the early morning, and so avoiding digestion time means I can train within 15 minutes of waking.
Training this way means I use stored carbohydrates and fat to provide fuel. There is a lot of discussion in the endurance community about this 'fat adapted approach to fueling and it is becoming increasingly more accepted.
Prior to my weekly long run, I have 40g of porridge and 30g of whey protein 2.5 hours. This meal, plus my body's stored energy will get me through 90minutes of high intensity exercise (up to 1/2 marathon).
This season I have been fueling my longer workouts (greater than 90 minutes) and races from half marathon upwards with UCAN. (www.ucan.co).

UCAN contains Superstarch, which is a complex carbohydrate that releases energy slowly to your system. As such it avoids the roller coaster blood sugar highs and lows associated with gels. It has some high profile advocates including 2014 Boston Marathon Champion Meb Keflezighi and Professional Ironman champion Tim O'Donnell.

My Boston race day nutrition plan was:

07:30 40g porridge mixed with water
09:30 One sachet UCAN Superstarch mixed with 500 mls water
10.00 Race start
11.30 Halfway – One sachet of UCAN Superstarch mixed as a gel
I did have some Lucozade Endurance at the mile 25 aid station which in retrospect I didn't need as it wouldn't have hit my system before I finished. Old habits die hard!

I had consistent energy throughout the race with no GI discomfort at all. This is the first race where I have never had any GI issues, so I am a believer in UCAN!

Marginal gains
There were 2 further areas that I focused on this year to optimize performance – body weight and recovery.

Body weight
Over the course of the 16 week course I dropped 10lbs, to reach my lightest racing weight of 11stone 8lbs (162 lbs.)
When I set my previous marathon PB my weight was 11st 12lbs (166lbs).
Over the course of a marathon, a 4lbs drop in body weight is predicted to be worth 3:47 mins.
Weight / Predicted time/ Time difference
162 lbs. 03:01:57 -03:47
163 lbs. 03:02:54 -02:50
164 lbs. 03:03:51 -01:53
165 lbs. 03:04:47 -00:57
166 lbs. 03:05:44
167 lbs. 03:06:41 +00:57
168 lbs. 03:07:37 +01:53

Recovery
I focused on optimizing my sleep quality and quantity and noticed a huge difference. The changes that I made were:
– No caffeinated tea/ coffee after 6pm at the latest
– Eating dinner earlier – average of 6pm compared with 8pm
– Supplementing with Magnesium 45 mins prior to bed

– Reading before bed and banning the iPhone from the bedroom

Summary
There is not one thing that I can pinpoint that has helped me to run better this year, rather I have found a formula of many things that have worked for me.
I hope there are some useful ideas for you to use here or at least get you thinking.
There are lots of you out there who have broken 3 hours and it would be great to know what tactics have worked for you and share 'best-practice'. If you would like to contribute to the conversation, you can contact me at https://paulbradfordcoaching.com/

Stay Strong
PB
April 27, 2015

New York Marathon Race Report - November 2016 (Time 2:58.32s)
Every day is a school day: Lessons from the NYC Marathon

For those looking to go sub-3, I'm in the process of publishing the system that I've developed to achieve this goal.

If you are interested in finding out more then please message me and I can let you know when it's available.

In the meantime, here are some key points I have learned from last Sunday's race.

Every challenging race that we do is an opportunity to learn and grow. I went sub-3 at the recent NYC marathon but the course really took me back to school and I learned some hard lessons. I'd like to share with you my top 3 takeaways that could not only be used to prepare for this course but for any marathon course:

1) Course knowledge is critical
2) Every step counts
3) Your Garmin lies

1) Course knowledge is critical

I knew that the course was hilly, and my long runs really focused on taking in big hills.

I reminded myself of the course profile by reading a couple of race reports the day before the race. This gave me a refreshed insight into how to strategically pace it, however I now know that this theoretical knowledge of the course is no substitute for actually doing it.

It's common in an Ironman buildup to recce the course in the days leading up to the event on a bike or car. This would have been virtually impossible in New York. It's simply not feasible to drive a hire car start-stop for 26.2 Miles in the Big Apple!

The result was that I didn't truly know what to expect until my feet hit the tarmac, and my concern about what lay around each turn grew increasingly from mile 20. What was revealed was that after 4 miles running straight up 1st Ave, Willis Avenue bridge reveals itself as the gateway to the Bronx. It's a short incline but feels crazy hard at this stage. After weaving though the Bronx and back into Manhattan it's 3 miles net uphill until you reach Central Park for the final 5km.

If I knew then what I know now, I would have backed off the pace up to mile 15 and saved some gas for the tough later stages.

I would advise anyone thinking off doing this course to try and seek out someone who has done it before. This could very well make the difference between holding it together or not in the latter stages of the race.

2) Every step counts

With the benefit of hindsight, I went too quickly up to mile 15. After negotiating the Queensboro bridge into Manhattan, my average pace started dropping but my effort level went up massively. I was starting to become inefficient, but most critically for the first time in the race I started to have doubts.

Have I gone off to fast? Probably

Should it feel this hard? No

Have I taken on enough fuel to get me to the end? ... I don't know

The most significant question that came into my now glycogen depleted brain was - Can I do this?

That is ultimately the only real question. All the other questions just roll up into this mother: Can I really do this?

I know now the answer is a resounding yes, and that I was in the physical shape to break 3 hours. What I also learned is that I have the mental fortitude to dig deeper than I ever thought possible.

This was a mental victory, not a physical one.

For any runner aspiring to hit a marathon time goal, the mental game is absolutely critical.

What kept me hammering was a single thought:

"Run an honest race."

To get to the end of any endeavor and to know that you gave everything is the real victory. Regardless of the outcome, when are alone and you can say to yourself that you gave absolutely everything that you had, then you've won the most important personal victory. I wanted to feel that I gave it all I had and that every step counted. I paced the uphill, raced the flats and downhills and didn't back off for 1 step over 26.2 miles.

In the end, all those 'all-in' steps added up to coming in under 3 hours. Marginal gains pay off.

3) Your Garmin lies

To achieve a sub-3 result the absolutely slowest pace I could average was 6.51 mins / mile. Just one more second slower per mile and I would have missed my goal by 3 seconds.

I knew that the from mile 15 onwards the course was lumpy and so I wanted to hit an average pace of 6.40 mins/mile by the time I hit the Queensboro bridge to give me a time-cushion. At this point I was slightly ahead at schedule at 6.38mins/mile. As I came off the bridge into Manhattan, that predicted slow mile had started to eat into my average pace. No sweat, that was part of the plan.

However, over the next few miles, my average pace continued to drop and after a dreadful patch between mile 23 and 24 it faded to 6.51min/mile. I'd blown it. My form was ragged and slowing. As I entered Central Park, I knew that all this effort would result in a time just seconds over 3 hours.

Then I clocked the official race clock, and a quick calculation of the remaining distance meant that I was still on track. It didn't add up. My Garmin says I've blown it, my fatigued brain is doing calculations to say I can do it.

What do to?

I hammered. I went all in, knowing I had just 15 minutes of suffering to go. The result was that my official pace was 6.49 min/ mile, yet my Garmin measured short at 25.99 miles and 6.51 mins / mile.

This is a critical lesson! Use your Garmin as a guide for pacing but also keep your race head switched on. Keep checking your splits. The finish line is where the organizers put it, not where your Garmin tells you.

Summary

Whether you achieve your goal or not, the opportunities are always there to learn and improve for the next challenge. I hope these 3 critical lessons can help you achieve your marathon goals.

Stay strong!

Paul

ABOUT THE AUTHOR

HUSBAND. FATHER. SON. BUSINESSMAN. COACH... **ATHLETE**

Since the age of 12 I have been fascinated with the science of performance, leading to my career as a physiotherapist. Following years of clinical work, I embarked on my career in the Medical Devices industry, focusing on making healthcare better, AND spending 50% of my time out of the country whilst balancing my life's other priorities.

Despite this challenging schedule, I have mastered time-efficient training principles to successfully compete as a:

- Bodybuilder (Northwest Britain Middleweight Champion)

- Marathon Runner (Sub-3 hour Finisher)

- Ironman Triathlete (Hawaii World Championship Qualifier)

In 2022, I suffered a severe traumatic brain injury whilst cycling. Incurring multiple fractures, my chance of survival was less than 10%.

I survived thanks to outstanding Medical Care **AND** because of my physical fitness.

My recovery prognosis was to return to 70-80% of previous-ability and that I would be off work for at least 12 months.

6 months later, I have returned to work and training 7 days a week.

Most Importantly I have returned to being husband and a father.

Throughout all this, my identity as an ATHLETE has never wavered.

I've learned so much, I am here to support others on their journey from adversity to high performance.

Stay Strong

Paul

(www.paulbradfordcoaching.com)

<u>NOTES</u>

Paul Bradford

<u>NOTES</u>

<u>NOTES</u>

<u>NOTES</u>

<u>NOTES</u>

<u>NOTES</u>

<u>NOTES</u>

Paul Bradford

<u>NOTES</u>

<u>NOTES</u>

Paul Bradford

<u>NOTES</u>

Made in the USA
Coppell, TX
13 March 2023

14204822R00046